URUGUAY

...in Pictures

Visual Geography Series®

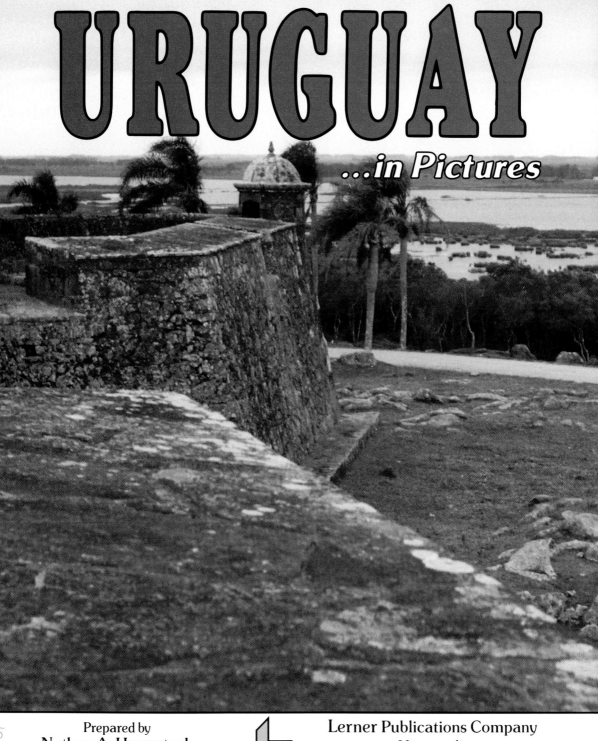

URUGUAY

...in Pictures

Prepared by
Nathan A. Haverstock

Lerner Publications Company
Minneapolis

12397

Top-quality wools from Uruguay's sheep are among the country's major exports.

This is an all-new edition of the Visual Geography Series. Previous editions have been published by Sterling Publishing Company, New York City, and some of the original textual information has been retained. New photographs, maps, charts, captions, and updated information have been added. The text has been entirely reset in 10/12 Century Textbook.

LIBRARY OF CONGRESS CATALOGING-IN-PUBLICATION DATA

> **Haverstock, Nathan A.**
>   Uruguay in pictures.
>
>   (Visual geography series)
>   Includes index.
>   Summary: Introduces the land, history, government, people, and economy of a small South American country.
>   1. Uruguay. [1. Uruguay] I. Title. II. Series: Visual geography series (Minneapolis, Minn.)
> F2708.H38   1987   989.5   87-3955
> ISBN 0-8225-1823-6 (lib. bdg.)

International Standard Book Number: 0-8225-1823-6
Library of Congress Catalog Card Number: 87-3955

VISUAL GEOGRAPHY SERIES®

Publisher
Harry Jonas Lerner
Associate Publisher
Nancy M. Campbell
Executive Series Editor
Mary M. Rodgers
Assistant Series Editor
Gretchen Bratvold
Editorial Assistant
Nora W. Kniskern
Illustrations Editors
Nathan A. Haverstock
Karen A. Sirvaitis
Consultants/Contributors
Dr. Ruth F. Hale
Nathan A. Haverstock
Sandra K. Davis
Designer
Jim Simondet
Cartographer
Carol F. Barrett
Indexer
Kristine S. Schubert
Production Manager
Richard J. Hannah

A monument to the gaucho, or cowboy, stands in front of the Commercial Bank in Montevideo.

Acknowledgments

Title page photo by Don Irish.

Elevation contours adapted from *The Times Atlas of the World*, seventh comprehensive edition (New York: Times Books, 1985).

2 3 4 5 6 7 8 9 10 97 96 95 94 93 92 91 90 89 88

As the price of single-family homes becomes more expensive, more families live in high-rise apartment complexes. The housing project where these children are playing is located on Avenida Centenario in suburban Montevideo.

Contents

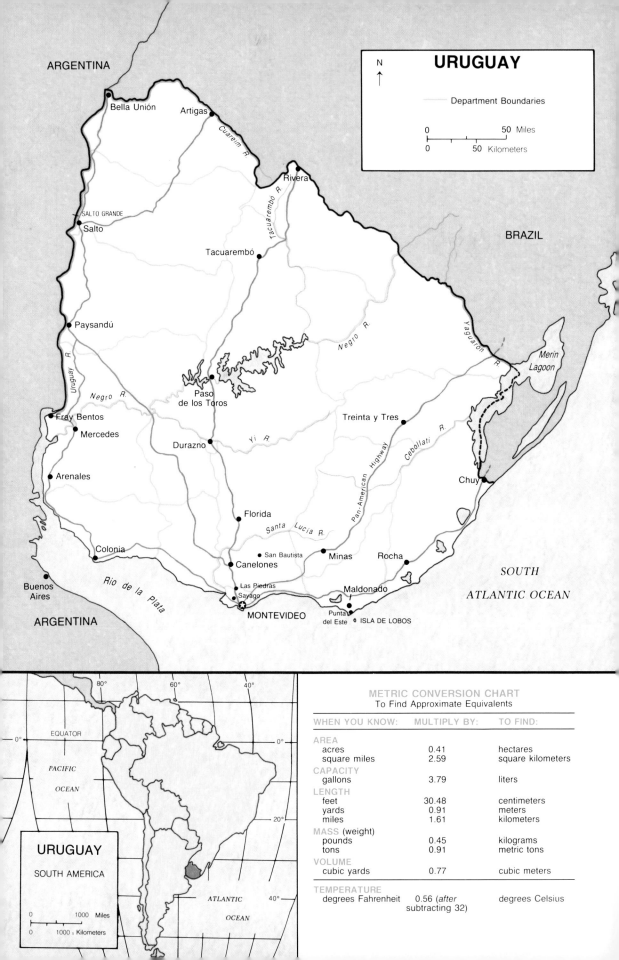

ARGENTINA

Bella Unión

Artigas

Cuareim R.

URUGUAY

N
↑

— Department Boundaries

0   50   Miles

0   50   Kilometers

Tacuarembó R.

Rivera

BRAZIL

SALTO GRANDE

Salto

Tacuarembó

Negro R.

Yaguarón R.

Merín
Lagoon

Paysandú

Uruguay R.

Paso
de los Toros

Negro R.

Yi R.

Treinta y Tres

Cebollati R.

Fray Bentos

Mercedes

Durazno

Pan-American Highway

Arenales

Chuy

Florida

Santa Lucia R.

Colonia

San Bautista

Minas

Rocha

SOUTH

Canelones

ATLANTIC OCEAN

Buenos
Aires

Río de la Plata

Las Piedras
Sayago

Maldonado

ARGENTINA

MONTEVIDEO

Punta
del Este   ISLA DE LOBOS

80°   60°   40°

EQUATOR

0°   0°

PACIFIC

OCEAN

20°

URUGUAY

SOUTH AMERICA

ATLANTIC

40°

OCEAN

0   1000   Miles

0   1000   Kilometers

METRIC CONVERSION CHART
To Find Approximate Equivalents

WHEN YOU KNOW:	MULTIPLY BY:	TO FIND:
AREA		
acres	0.41	hectares
square miles	2.59	square kilometers
CAPACITY		
gallons	3.79	liters
LENGTH		
feet	30.48	centimeters
yards	0.91	meters
miles	1.61	kilometers
MASS (weight)		
pounds	0.45	kilograms
tons	0.91	metric tons
VOLUME		
cubic yards	0.77	cubic meters
TEMPERATURE		
degrees Fahrenheit	0.56 (*after* subtracting 32)	degrees Celsius

These Uruguayan farm laborers work on citrus fields near Paysandú, where they load their recent harvest of grapefruits, oranges, and tangerines.

Introduction

Uruguay owes its independence as a nation to rivalries between its powerful neighbors, Brazil and Argentina, and to the desire of New World peoples to keep South America free of European—especially British—imperialism. Uruguay has played the quiet and unassuming role of the neutral neighbor. Standing as a buffer between these two political and commercial rivals, Uruguay has found it wise to practice moderation in all things—from lifestyles to politics—while quietly developing the resources of its farms and ranches.

At one time this approach worked well for Uruguay, where a steady flow of hard-working European immigrants had settled and created one of the best-educated and best-fed peoples of the Americas. Uruguay became an overwhelmingly middle-class country, where there was enough for all and where the fruits of labor were distributed fairly among the people. Political matters were resolved through a highly democratic system of government. Broad-based, national interests were accurately reflected by two political parties—one

7

speaking for the liberal views of those who lived in the capital city of Montevideo, the other speaking for the conservative outlook of those who lived on farms and ranches.

Both parties produced capable and honest leaders who were dedicated to serving the people and who freely mingled with them in everyday life. Uruguay created a society that embodied much of the ideal of universal social justice well before most nations of the Americas—including the United States—attempted to do so.

By 1907 Uruguay had a law permitting women to sue for divorce on the grounds of cruelty. By 1915 an eight-hour workday was the law in Uruguay, and programs were already in place for social security, rural credit, and health care—programs that would become models for the U.S.

Photo by Don Irish

The Gran Hotel Colón—graced with Spanish-style architecture—is located in the older section of Montevideo, Uruguay's capital city.

New Deal of the 1930s. By 1919 José Batlle y Ordóñez had persuaded the nation's legislature to adopt a law providing for a form of government in which authority would be shared equally among several leaders. For his efforts, Batlle is still revered in Uruguay as the father of far-reaching welfare legislation.

Like farmers of the U.S. midwest, Uruguayans have been hurt by declining profits from agriculture. As farms and ranches have improved their large-scale production technology to achieve competitive efficiency, they no longer can employ as many workers. With shrinking profits and increasing unemployment, Uruguay's farmers can no longer bear the burden of supporting social programs once hailed as the most progressive in the world.

As Uruguay's economy declined further, a terrorist group arose in the 1960s that sought to reestablish the old order but whose platform did not explain convincingly how this was to be accomplished. Uruguay's armed forces were strengthened to handle the terrorist menace, and, as often happens in such situations, not only triumphed over the terrorism but also became the dominant political force. In 1973, amid increasing economic and political troubles, Uruguay's armed forces closed down the congress and established a military dictatorship. Twelve years later, on February 15, 1985, the people restored democracy by electing a president and a congress.

Meanwhile the well-educated sons and daughters of Uruguay have increasingly gone to seek their fortunes elsewhere. Some 300,000 to 500,000 immigrant children—many of them packing the same trunks their parents used in coming to the New World—have gone elsewhere in search of economic opportunity. Some have settled in Buenos Aires across the Río de la Plata, others in the fast-industrializing cities of Pôrto Alegre or São Paulo in Brazil. Many will spend their working years in these places.

Much of Uruguay's grassy terrain provides natural pasture for grazing sheep.

1) The Land

Uruguay, with 63,037 square miles, is the second smallest independent nation of South America (after Suriname). Uruguay is similar in size and population to the U.S. state of Oklahoma. At its greatest width, from the northwest corner to the southeast Atlantic coast, the country measures only about 360 miles. Uruguay is a compact, pear-shaped country with no natural obstacles—mountains, deserts, or jungles —to hinder the development of the land.

The nation is called the Eastern Republic of Uruguay, because it lies on the eastern bank of the Uruguay River. This river forms the boundary with Argentina for 270 miles before it empties into the broad Río de la Plata—where fresh and ocean waters commingle.

A wide and useful estuary that forms Uruguay's southern boundary for 235 miles, the Río de la Plata and its tributaries drain about one-third of South America. The waterway provides Uruguay with easy access to the South Atlantic. Oceangoing vessels navigate the Río de la Plata to unload their cargoes at the port of Montevideo, Uruguay's capital and most important city.

Many fine beaches, peaceful lagoons, and windswept dunes mark Uruguay's southeastern border along 120 miles of Atlantic coastline. To complete the circuit of Uruguay's boundaries, the nation's northeastern frontier with Brazil is formed by the Merín Lagoon, by low-lying hills and ridges, and by the Cuareim and Yaguarón rivers.

Wildflowers add a bluish tinge to the lowlands above the Negro River near Paso de los Toros.

Topography

Fertile and rolling grasslands are the dominant feature of Uruguay's landscape. The many prosperous cattle ranges and croplands of Uruguay provide a welcome transition between the subtropical uplands and plateaus of southern Brazil and the hot, humid lowlands of northern Argentina. Although these lowlands extend into the northwestern quarter of Uruguay, they are less humid than in Argentina and form a fertile, level strip of land where cattle thrive. The lowlands of Uruguay eventually merge with a wide coastal plain that extends east from Montevideo to Maldonado and north to the Brazilian border.

The interior of Uruguay is mainly an area of gently rolling grasslands where

Uruguay's vast expanses of level land are well suited to the cultivation of grains—which are either used as fodder for the nation's all-important livestock or further refined into cereals and flours. Seen here is a broad field of wheat after the grain has been cut and stacked.

meat and wool—the nation's two most important products—are produced. The even sweep of the land is interrupted at two points by hilly ridges, called *cuchillas,* which are composed of granite formations that stick up like blades of knives. The Cuchilla de Haedo lies in the northwest, and the Cuchilla Grande extends northeast from near Montevideo to the Brazilian border. Neither of these ridges reaches an elevation of more than 1,500 to 2,000 feet, but they have rugged crests that were formed when weathered granite broke through the soil of the country's eastern and southern zones.

From the Cuchilla Grande, the terrain slopes gradually westward to the Uruguay River. The northwestern corner of the country is an extension of the southernmost portion of Brazil's Paraná Plateau. In prehistoric times, dark flows of lava covered much of the existing granite. These volcanic intrusions in Uruguay are set off from the adjoining lands by cuestas, or sharp cliffs with flat tops and steep, angular sides.

Rivers and Lagoons

The numerous rivers of Uruguay serve a vital economic role by draining the nation's productive grasslands. Most are navigable and provide direct access to the sea for Uruguay's exports. Along their banks, narrow ribbons of forest crisscross the country. The Negro River is the largest of the nation's inland waterways and is used by coastal shipping for about 45 miles inland. The lowlands along the Negro River widen into a large expanse of forest at the point where the river enters the Uruguay River. From its source in Brazil, the Negro River divides Uruguay in two along a northeast-southwest axis. The Tacuarembó River enters the Negro River at the end of an 87-mile-long lake formed when the Negro was dammed in the 1940s to create hydroelectric power.

Photo by Don Irish

Eucalyptus trees line the shores of Merín Lagoon—the largest of Uruguay's eastern coastal lagoons.

These workers are harvesting rice in a wet, low plain near the Merín Lagoon, which forms part of Uruguay's northeastern border with Brazil.

Uruguay's second most important river, the Yi—a tributary of the Negro River—rises in the hills of the Cuchilla Grande and flows for 140 miles. Other rivers and streams that begin in the Cuchilla Grande, such as the Cebollatí River, run eastward along shallow courses before feeding either into lagoons near the Atlantic coast or directly into the sea.

Both freshwater and saltwater lagoons thrive along Uruguay's Atlantic coast. A dozen or more of these lagoons have sur-face areas ranging from 15 to 70 square miles, and numerous smaller lagoons dot the coast.

Climate

Like Uruguay's gently rolling countryside, the climate is mild and fairly uniform. Because of the moderating effect of ocean breezes, temperature variance is not great. About one-third of the days are sunny, often with considerable humidity, particu-

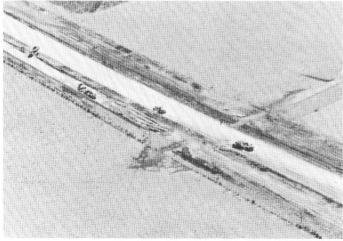

The flatness of much of Uruguay's land makes it easy to build roads. Here, workers pave a stretch between Paysandú and Tacuarembó.

larly during the midwinter months of July and August. (Because Uruguay is in the Southern Hemisphere, its seasons occur inversely to those of the Northern Hemisphere.)

Winter temperatures range around 57° to 60° F. Though occasionally temperatures may drop as low as the mid-twenties, it rarely snows. Summer temperatures average about 75° F. Uruguay's mild summer weather, however, often changes unpredictably—a warm sunny afternoon can be interrupted by looming clouds and cold southern winds that bring with them a sharp drop in temperature.

In the south, Montevideo receives about 40 inches of rainfall a year, while about 50 inches fall in the north. Rainfall decreases somewhat as it moves inland from the coast. Though the volume of Uruguay's rainfall is dependable, the nation's farmers and ranchers anxiously watch the skies, hoping that the rain will fall when they need it. Normally, the rain falls most frequently in the winter, but the heaviest storms occur in the autumn, and summer thunderstorms are also common.

Uruguay has the distinction of being the only Latin American country that lies wholly outside of the tropics. Its location within the middle latitudes, or temperate zone, has played an important role in shaping the economy and the character of both Uruguay and its people.

Grasslands and Forests

Only 3 percent of Uruguay is covered with native forests. Most of the country has grazing lands suited to all kinds of livestock. Because of the importance of livestock to the Uruguayan economy, some of the country's native grasslands have been replaced with imported grasses that have a higher nutrient value as feed for animals than do the native grasses.

Three-fourths of Uruguay's land consists of level areas broken only by gentle hills and hollows—ideal pasture for grazing the cattle that provide both Uruguayan and foreign markets with top-quality beef.

In the springtime many wildflowers, including verbena, mix with Uruguay's native prairie grasses, giving the countryside a soft, pastel glow.

Montevideo's oldest park, El Prado, is famous for its zoo, museums, rose gardens, fine lawns, fountains, and artificial lakes.

But whether the grasses are native or imported, in the spring the rural landscape of Uruguay boasts an abundance of wild-flowers. The flowers of a native species of verbena often give a lavender cast to wide areas of the grasslands. It was the verbena, with its showy clusters of flowers, that inspired the British writer and naturalist William Henry Hudson to call his widely read work *The Purple Land That England Lost.*

Uruguay has few kinds of trees compared to heavily forested Brazil to the north. The trees of Uruguay are those commonly found in temperate zones, except in the far northwest where forest growth is thick and dense, and tropical orchids cling to tree trunks and branches.

Among the trees native to the country are the willow, acacia, myrtle, and laurel. Lignum vitae, a prized hardwood, and quebracho, whose bark is used in tanning leather, grow well in Uruguay's soil. Several temperate-zone trees not native to Uruguay have been introduced and have adapted to the environment. Eucalyptus trees have been brought from Australia, and poplars line roadways and surround ranchers' homes. Pines have been planted behind the Atlantic beaches to help stabilize the soil and prevent sand dunes from creeping inland.

A wide range of fruit and nut trees has been introduced, and most have done well commercially. These include peach, pear, and apple trees, various citrus trees—lemon, orange, and grapefruit—as well as olive, almond, date, and banana trees. At Rocha in southeastern Uruguay, a belt of tropical palms extends across the country, which some say marks a primitive trade route dating back before the time of Columbus.

Courtesy of Inter-American Development Bank

This farmhand harvests oranges at the Sandupay Company, a large agribusiness near Paysandú. Grapefruits and tangerines are also cultivated on the 5,000-acre plantation, and about half of the total production is exported to Europe.

Photo by Don Irish

Orange trees and tropical palms flourish at this park in Colonia, a port city on the Río de la Plata.

15

Easily the most striking tree is the ombu, whose thick, ungainly trunk is depicted in early prints and paintings of Uruguay. Though the huge trunks of this tree are too pulpy to be used for construction or as fuel, the leaves provide welcome shade in areas devoid of other trees—and the ombu itself has become prominent in Uruguayan folklore.

Wildlife

Uruguay has few four-footed animals. Of the animals once native to the country—including pumas (mountain lions), jaguars, and wildcats—most have long since been hunted to extinction. Deer, fox, and the carpincho, a South American water hog, are occasionally seen. The mulita, a small armadillo, survives in the northern hills, and the nutria, an aquatic rodent with beaverlike fur, is commercially valuable.

Fur-bearing seals, whose hides are highly prized, inhabit the Isla de Lobos, a rocky island off the Atlantic coast near Punta del Este. The island boasts the Southern Hemisphere's most important seal-breeding ground—a sanctuary strictly controlled and protected by Uruguayan authorities.

Uruguay's birdlife is rich and varied. Flightless antarctic penguins reach Uruguayan beaches by swimming the cold currents of water that circulate north from polar regions. Another flightless bird, the rhea, or South American ostrich, runs with giant strides across the nation's open plains. Years ago, ostrich plumes were a significant Uruguayan export, shipped overseas to decorate fashionable ladies' hats.

Independent Picture Service

These seals on Isla de Lobos have been skinned for their valuable furs. The Uruguayan government carefully regulates the fur industry, in order to prevent overkilling of the animals.

Two young boys enjoy watching a group of male seals. When on land, seals move slowly by wriggling and hunching the entire body.

Ocean birds are plentiful, as well as marsh and wading birds—including various kinds of snipes and plovers. Inland, parakeets are common, and the open lands and pastures abound with small quail-like partridges and less numerous prairie hens, both of which are still widely hunted. Ovenbirds build mud nests on the tops of fence posts and telegraph poles. Another striking native bird, whose name is derived from its cry, is the crow-sized teruterú—a bird with dramatic black-and-white bands and a sharp spur on the leading edge of each wing.

Although Uruguay is not a challenging source of sport for the hunter, the country is a fisherman's paradise. The waters of its southeastern coast provide one of the world's major fishing grounds. Most numerous among the species found in Uruguay's ocean waters are black bass, mackerel, tuna, hake, mullet, sole, whiting, and anchovy. Surf fishermen cast from jetties on the beach for bluefish, weakfish, and drum—so called because it makes a drumming noise. Uruguay's rivers—especially those near the town of Paysandú—are home to the dorado (literally "golden one"), a salmonlike fish that averages 30 pounds but may weigh up to 60 pounds.

Natural Resources

Uruguay's principal physical resource is the black, potash-rich soil on which more than 9 million head of cattle and nearly 22 million sheep graze. Nearly 80 percent of the entire nation is given over to pastureland, with an additional 10 percent devoted to the cultivation of temperate-zone crops. Hence, nearly all of Uruguay's land is put to agricultural use.

Uruguay has neither coal nor petroleum in appreciable quantities. The lack of these sources of energy has held back the development of industry. Recently a fairly high grade of iron ore was discovered in the central part of the country. Small amounts of manganese, copper, lead, and gold can be found—but not enough to provide the basis for a mining industry. The nation does, however, have numerous marble quarries, and this beautiful stone of many hues and textures is used both at home and abroad in fine construction. Uruguay also exports some granite, limestone, talc, and sand.

Cities and Towns

Roughly half of Uruguay's population lives in the metropolitan area of Montevideo —the capital city. Founded in 1726, Montevideo soon became Uruguay's chief seaport, center of colonial administration, and bastion of defense against the encroachments of others—most notably the Portuguese. The capital became a lively commercial town, with its own shopkeepers, merchants, lawyers, and doctors.

By far the largest city in Uruguay, Montevideo has a population estimated at 1.35 million.

Photo by Maria Moline

The capital today boasts a main thoroughfare that is lined with an intriguing mix of old buildings alongside modern, high-rise office buildings. The side streets are full of modest shops and business establishments.

The old port district of Montevideo has narrow streets, fine colonial-era houses, and office buildings—some of them in the process of restoration. The old market, a huge iron-framed building, is a storehouse brimming with fresh bread, cheese, meats, and fish.

Montevideo has many attractive parks and open spaces. It is largely free of slums, partly because Uruguay has few desperately poor people. Moreover, families tend to be small, and the nation's population

Courtesy of Inter-American Development Bank

Uruguay's center of culture and commerce, the port city of Montevideo handles most of the country's imports and exports.

Independent Picture Service

The extravagantly designed Palacio Salvo—which originally served as a hotel but now houses offices and apartments—remains one of Montevideo's landmarks.

cial mention should be made of Punta del Este, the country's leading pleasure resort. Located on the Atlantic coast, a little more than an hour by car from Montevideo, Punta del Este has served as a conference site for major inter-American meetings in recent years—a point of national pride.

Paysandú and Salto, important secondary ports, have populations of about 70,000 each. The inland towns of Mercedes and Rivera, with populations of 35,000 and 50,000 respectively, serve as business centers. Other towns of note include Fray Bentos, a meat-packing hub with a population of 20,000; Canelones, a suburb of the capital with a population of 15,000; and Maldonado, a colonial town on the Atlantic coast that was once a pirate stronghold, now with a population of 25,000.

In contrast to Montevideo, the rural towns and villages of Uruguay are quiet places that exist mainly as supply depots for the outlying ranches and farms. Rural towns are located on well-paved roads that fan out from the capital, and the commerce of the countryside thus easily flows toward Montevideo.

has remained fairly stable throughout most of the twentieth century.

No other city in Uruguay is even remotely comparable to Montevideo, though spe-

Photo by Don Irish

The seats of this open-air theater in the port city of Fray Bentos command an impressive view of the Uruguay River.

Montevideo, as depicted by an artist in 1861, was a bustling center of commerce.

2) History and Government

Without gold, silver, or precious stones to attract greedy eyes, Uruguay was largely untouched by Spain's New World conquerors. Whereas the native inhabitants in other places in the Americas were forced to work in the mines to increase Spain's wealth, Uruguay's Indians were left to enjoy their ancestral lands. Eventually, the Spanish crown did send missionaries to convert the Indians of Uruguay to Christianity. Fortunately, however, Spain did not impose feudal systems for working the land—probably because the region's agricultural richness did not require them.

Early Explorers

Throughout its history Uruguay has had the advantage of being somewhat removed from well-traveled paths, which has aided its development as a self-reliant and independent nation. During the sixteenth century, a few New World explorers did stop off briefly in Uruguay while looking in vain along the Río de la Plata for a water passage through the heart of the continent to the Pacific Ocean. The first of them, Juan de Solís, dropped anchor in 1516 just a short distance from the present site of Montevideo.

Pleased with what he saw, Solís ordered his armed party to put ashore, but he and his men were quickly overpowered by the fierce Charrúa Indians. There on the beach, the cannibals built fires and devoured the hapless explorer and his men. The only survivor was a cabin boy—who managed to live on among the Indians until his rescue a dozen years later.

In 1520 Ferdinand Magellan—a Portuguese captain in the service of Spain and the first person to lead an expedition to sail around the world—traveled along the south coast of Uruguay. Like Solís, Magellan was looking for a passage to the Pacific. According to popular legend, when

Sculpted in bronze by José Luis Zorilla de San Martín, *El Ultimo Charrúa* (The Last Charrúa) can be seen in Montevideo's El Prado Park.

one of Magellan's lookouts saw the site of the present-day Uruguayan capital from the crow's nest he cried out, *"Monte vide eu!"* ("I see a mountain!" in Portuguese), thus giving the place its future name.

Seven years later Sebastian Cabot—an Englishman in the service of Spain—sailed to the Uruguayan coast and found the surviving cabin boy who was by then a young man. Cabot was pleased to have the lad as an interpreter to communicate with the Indians in their own tongue, and the youth was overjoyed to be rescued. It was on this visit that Cabot gave the Río de la Plata, or River of Silver, its name. Whether the explorer was inspired by the silvery shimmering surface of the water or by the mistaken notion that the banks of the river were rich in silver deposits remains uncertain.

Little is known of Uruguay during the remainder of the sixteenth century. Beginning in 1580 the thrones of Portugal and Spain were united for 60 years, thus eliminating a source of Old World rivalry for Uruguay's territory. The Charrúa Indians —for the most part left undisturbed— rarely needed to repel intruders with their clubs, spears, bows and arrows, and bolas, or "stone-throwers."

Cowboys and Missionaries

The next century, however, found the peace of the Indians permanently disrupted by the arrival of cattle raisers and missionaries. Hernando Arias, first governor of nearby Paraguay, is generally credited as the one who introduced ranching into Uruguay. Arias, while shipping some cattle

Hernando Arias, who introduced horses and cattle to Uruguay, is commemorated in this statue on Montevideo's waterfront.

and horses downstream through Uruguay, turned them loose to run wild on the territory's native pastures. The animals thrived and multiplied rapidly on the abundant grasslands. Soon the herds of these undomesticated creatures attracted the attention of gauchos, or cowboys, who lived across the Río de la Plata in the increasingly well settled area around Buenos Aires.

The rugged gauchos, who eventually became heroic figures in the literature and folklore of the area, were independent individuals. Having no permanent abodes, they cared little for titles to land or for the development of settled communities. They preferred simply to follow the cattle herds—slaughtering the beasts for food and using their hides for clothing.

In 1624 Jesuit and Franciscan missionaries followed the gauchos, not to herd cattle, but to lead the Charrúa into villages, where the Indians were taught Western habits and were assembled as a captive audience to hear sermons on the Christian way of life. The missionaries succeeded in Christianizing the Charrúa and in extend-

Now restored and converted into a museum, the colonial fortress of Santa Teresa *(above and below)* on the northeastern coast of Uruguay was built by the Spanish in the 1760s to resist Portuguese invasions.

ing Spanish culture and influence. They also stored up wealth for themselves and their religious orders—something that would eventually lead to their undoing.

During most of the eighteenth century, the settlement of Uruguay continued—

with neither help nor hindrance from Spain. Spain's presence was mainly represented by priests. In promoting Christianity and Spanish culture, the work of the missionaries was facilitated by Uruguay's open grasslands and lack of remote jungles and mountains where unwilling Indians might have hidden from the Europeans. Instead, with Christian ways and clothes, the Indians were soon absorbed into the more numerous immigrant population. The Charrúa Indians proved to be strong and valuable workers on the cattle estates.

With the founding of Montevideo in 1726, pressures increased to free the colony of Uruguay from the oppressive influence of church officials—many of whom had grown extremely wealthy. In 1767, in response to the growth of local enterprise and initiative, the Spanish crown expelled the Jesuit priests, a group that many felt had grown too big and too successful.

From that moment the Roman Catholic missions in Uruguay entered a period of decline, from which they were never to recover.

Rivalry with Portugal

In the mid-seventeenth century, when the crowns of Spain and Portugal once again separated, an intense rivalry began within the region of the Río de la Plata for the surrounding territory and trade. As if to defy Spanish claims, the Portuguese established a settlement in 1680 at Colonia, directly across the Río de la Plata from the Spanish settlement at Buenos Aires.

Because Colonia threatened Spain's monopoly over an increasingly profitable river trade, Spain at once sent troops to capture and occupy the town. This incident sparked a feud that set Spain and Portugal intermittently at odds with one another for the next century and a half.

Dedicated to the pioneers of Uruguay, *La Carreta* (The Two-wheeled Cart) is a bronze grouping of three yokes of oxen drawing a covered wagon, followed by a bearded horseman and two free oxen. Located in Montevideo's Batlle Park, the life-sized sculpture was created by Uruguayan artist José Belloni.

Three-hundred-year-old historic ruins still stand at Colonia—a small town on the Río de la Plata founded by Portuguese settlers from Brazil in 1680.

Though Portugal regained control of Colonia in 1763, 14 years later Spain took permanent possession of the town and, along with it, had enduring influence within the territory of modern Uruguay. In 1776 Spain's Bourbon monarchs began tightening up administration within their empire. They created a new viceroyalty of the Río de la Plata area and strengthened the region's military defenses.

Viceroyalty of La Plata

In addition to the present-day territory of Argentina, the new viceroyalty—with headquarters in Buenos Aires—embraced the area of modern Paraguay and Uruguay and parts of Bolivia, Brazil, and Chile. Uruguay and its capital of Montevideo were thus reduced to a subordinate status, and Uruguayans were resentful of this demotion. Their resentment smoldered for the next two decades until, toward the end of the eighteenth century, Spain and Great Britain were at war. As the conflict developed, the British fleet exercised a clear-cut supremacy over the aging Spanish flotillas.

The British occupied Buenos Aires in 1807 and Montevideo in 1808—the year when Napoleon Bonaparte and his armies overran Spain, imprisoned Spain's king

Ferdinand VII, and placed Napoleon's brother Joseph on the Spanish throne. Settlers in Uruguay, as elsewhere in Spanish America, were divided in their loyalties. Some pledged their allegiance to Ferdinand —Spain's rightful sovereign—and others supported Joseph Bonaparte.

José Artigas

The rise of José Gervasio Artigas and the Uruguayan independence movement occurred amid Uruguayan anger over the mismanagement of their homeland by far-off authorities in Spain. Son of a Montevideo family, Artigas had adopted the gaucho way of life. He opposed the Spanish administration in Buenos Aires, especially its discrimination against Montevideo's trade. He thought deeply about the situation of his country, and he nourished his opinions by reading such publications as *Common Sense* and *The Rights of Man,* written by the North American Thomas Paine. Though these works were considered dangerous by Spanish authorities, Artigas had managed to secure them in Spanish translation.

Artigas organized an army of gaucho forces and in 1811 laid seige to Monte-

José Gervasio Artigas, a patriot and gaucho from Montevideo who became the leader of the independence movement, led Uruguayans in revolt against Spain in 1811.

video, the seat of Spanish rule in Uruguay. Portuguese troops from Brazil intervened —trying to gain Uruguay for themselves.

The Uruguayan painter Zorilla de San Martín has depicted Artigas negotiating a commercial treaty with the British.

In response Artigas led an exodus of about 15,000 Uruguayans—one-fourth of the total population—to the west bank of the Uruguay River in neighboring Argentina and Paraguay.

For two years Artigas refused to submit to the control of Spanish authorities in Buenos Aires. His price, which Buenos Aires rejected in 1813, was a guarantee of complete autonomy for Uruguay. Buenos Aires troops took Montevideo in 1814, but Artigas and his gauchos drove them out in 1815 and declared independence. The rebels set up a federal republic patterned after the United States and held together a large federated area—including not only the Banda Oriental, or eastern bank of the Río de la Plata, but the northern provinces of Argentina as well.

In 1816 Artigas was driven out of Uruguay by new, larger, and stronger Portuguese forces from Brazil. Artigas withdrew to the northern Argentine provinces, where he continued to oppose the Buenos Aires central government. When he was finally defeated in 1820, Artigas sought sanctuary in Paraguay, where he lived in poverty for 30 years. Admirers of Artigas say that through his heroic deeds he created a Uruguayan sense of national pride and laid the foundation for the country's independent existence.

Given Uruguay's geographical location —across the river from Buenos Aires, southern South America's foremost city, and south of Brazil, the continent's biggest nation—Artigas's accomplishments are even more striking. Had it not been for Artigas, present-day Uruguay would surely have become part of either Argentina or Brazil. That Uruguay survived into nationhood at all is largely due to the jealousies of European powers anxious to absorb as big a portion as possible of the Río de la Plata region. Uruguay's independence is also due to the rivalry—which still continues—between Argentina and Brazil. Throughout its history, Uruguay has survived mainly by serving as a buffer state

—that is, by tempering and limiting contact between the two bigger nations.

The 33 Immortals

Before Artigas could complete his mission, Brazil annexed the Banda Oriental. Brazilian rule was mild enough, but the Uruguayans' newfound pride suffered. In 1825 a group of Uruguayan exiles living in Buenos Aires invaded their homeland.

Known to history as the 33 Immortals, the rebels—under the leadership of Juan Antonio Lavalleja and José Fructuoso Rivera—mounted an impressive revolt. The local population was quick to rally to their banner. Moreover, the authorities in

Photo by Don Irish

A bronze equestrian statue of Juan Antonio Lavalleja—coleader of the 33 Immortals who brought independence to Uruguay—adorns the public square in the town of Minas.

27

Independent Picture Service

In a period painting, Uruguay's 33 Immortals swear allegiance to their homeland. Their successful campaign to win freedom for Uruguay began in 1825.

Buenos Aires, seeing a chance to incorporate the Banda Oriental into their sphere of influence, sent land and naval forces to help the rebels.

Argentine intervention brought war between Argentina and Brazil, with the Brazilians subjecting Buenos Aires to a tight and effective naval blockade. The blockade put a virtual stop to Great Britain's trade in the area, and British diplomats in 1828 succeeded in negotiating a settlement between the two warring South American rivals. As part of the settlement, Uruguay was designated as a buffer between Argentina and Brazil. From this negotiated beginning, Uruguay has maintained its independence—though at times somewhat precariously—ever since.

Rich in dramatic style and realism, *The Two Ways*—by nineteenth-century Uruguayan artist Juan Manuel Blanes—depicts two gauchos at a crossroads.

Courtesy of Organization of American States

Nationhood

At the time of its creation as a nation, Uruguay's prospects were scarcely promising. The land was nearly deserted, with fewer than 100,000 people. Most were either gauchos, who managed the land and their cattle in a Wild-West style, or shepherds, who tended flocks of sheep scattered about the nation's grasslands. Only in the capital city was there a group of people with more than the barest essentials of education, and this constituted an unrepresentative elite. Yet it was precisely this group that had to wrestle with the problem of creating a nation.

On July 18, 1830, Uruguay enacted its first constitution. The drafters either did their job exceedingly well, or their successors had neither inclination nor skill to do better. This first constitution remained in effect for 89 years—a remarkable record considering the frequency with which constitutions were scrapped and rewritten in other South American republics.

One probable reason for the survival of the Uruguayan constitution was the freedom that it allowed. Local political groups could revise and modernize public institutions as well as reapportion power as realignments occurred within the nation's parties. In addition, Uruguay's leaders were zealous protectors of free speech within the nation's parliament—even when legislators voiced views directly opposed to those of the executive branch.

For the next 70 years Uruguay's continued existence was threatened by nearby countries and by internal strife. Perhaps as a strengthening measure, the nation soon adopted a two-party system of politics and government. By 1836 two well-defined parties, each with its own private gaucho army, had grown up around former leaders of the rebellious 33 Immortals. Manuel Oribe became the chief of a group of conservatives called Blancos, or Whites, because of the white ribbons they wore on their hatbands for identification. Their

Eighteenth of July Avenue runs into Plaza Independencia in this 1865 street scene.

At Plaza del Entrevero in Montevideo, this statue *(right and below)* by Uruguayan sculptor José Luis Zorilla de San Martín depicts a group of gauchos engaged in battle.

opponents, led by José Fructuoso Rivera, wore red ribbons and were called the Colorados, or Reds.

A New Troy

The rivalry of the Blancos and Colorados, which continues to this day, has been periodically complicated by the meddlesome interventions of other nations. In 1843, for example, the Argentine dictator Manuel Rosas supported the Blancos and thereby helped touch off an eight-and-a-half-year struggle, known in local history as the Great War.

The fighting included a prolonged Argentine siege of Montevideo, which was held by the Colorados. The Blancos, aided by the Argentines, imposed a naval blockade and intermittent land assaults. In Paris the Uruguayan struggle inspired the great French writer Alexandre Dumas—in a book called *Montevideo: A New Troy*—to compare the lot of the Uruguayan capital to that of ancient Troy, long ago laid siege by the Greeks.

Besides becoming the focus of international attention, the war took on the proportions of a civil war in Argentina as well as in Uruguay, with the opposing sides

The School of Law *(above)* is one of many departments at the University of the Republic, founded in 1849 in Montevideo. This and earlier views of the law school *(right)* and of the School of Medicine *(below)* – also in Montevideo – reflect the massive, ornate style of the late nineteenth century.

Courtesy of Organization of American States

The battlefront of the War of the Triple Alliance—in which the forces of Uruguay, Brazil, and Argentina joined against Paraguay—is depicted in this historical painting.

either for or against the tyrant Rosas. Arriving from Italy, Giuseppe Garibaldi— one of the founders of the modern nation of Italy—won a hero's laurels for his part in toppling Rosas during an Argentine uprising in 1851.

Revolutionary Strife

With the signing of a peace treaty on October 8, 1851, Uruguay found domestic tranquillity short-lived. Twice during the next 16 years, President Venancio Flores of the Colorado party had to request Brazilian help to maintain himself in office. In return for this help, Flores committed Uruguay to join with Argentina and Brazil from 1865 to 1870 in the War of the Triple Alliance against heavily armed, but hopelessly overpowered, Paraguay.

No sooner was this conflict over than Uruguay was torn once again by internal

Independent Picture Service

The war against Paraguay lasted six years, until the Paraguayan dictator Francisco Solano López was killed. Here, the raising of the white flag of truce ends the war, while Uruguay's Florida battalion pays its respects to its commander, who has just fallen in battle.

strife. The Colorados easily emerged the winners, and by 1872 it had become apparent that they were strong enough to maintain their political hold indefinitely. Widespread acceptance of this fact led both Colorado and Blanco civil and military leaders to strike a deal. The Blancos were given control of key public offices and local police forces in four of the country's nine departments (provinces), while the Colorados were allowed to dominate the balance of the departments and to run the national government. Following a brief uprising in 1897, Blanco control was increased to include six departments.

This arrangement provided the basic organization of Uruguay's two-party system, which through the years has seen the conservative Blanco party dominant among rural-based ranchers, and the more liberal Colorado party dominant in the cities, especially in Montevideo.

While this system for exercising national and local power was being hammered out, Uruguay itself was changing. In the latter decades of the nineteenth century, revolutionary violence subsided, and the nation's leaders succeeded each other peacefully. In contrast to the earlier rough-hewn gaucho caudillos, or political strongmen, more and more of Uruguay's presidents and ranking public officials were regular army officers.

The Late Nineteenth Century

During the late nineteenth century, social and political changes were accelerated by heavy immigration from Europe, particularly from Italy. The immigrants and their families—many of them skilled workers hailing from countries with well-defined political traditions—made a marked contribution to Uruguayan life. They demanded improvements in the country's schools, they increased the nation's productivity, and they added a fresh measure of social awareness to both of Uruguay's political parties.

If there was a single turning point in Uruguay's struggle for stability, it was perhaps the accord that followed the assassination of President Juan Idiarte Borda in 1897. Idiarte Borda—a Colorado with dictatorial tendencies—relied on the army for support, which led to civil war. Upon his death, leaders of both political parties laid down their arms and signed an agreement that guaranteed the political rights of all citizens.

The incoming Colorado president, Juan Lindolfo Cuestas, made the achievement of domestic peace his highest priority and put an end to the civil strife that had hindered productivity on the nation's farms. Uruguayans, who had seen or participated in some 50 revolutions in the previous 70 years, breathed easier. Finally, with the national spirit of harmony following the death of Idiarte Borda, there was hope. Besides resolving their disagreements, Uruguay's feuding parties had

Independent Picture Service

In 1900 Montevideo was a provincial capital, with low buildings and open, tranquil parks—such as the Plaza Constitución.

33

perhaps unwittingly created an atmosphere in which the nation's leaders could work toward defining Uruguayan solutions to Uruguayan problems.

José Batlle y Ordóñez

As the nation's political situation improved, José Batlle y Ordóñez appeared on the scene. Son of a former president of Uruguay, Batlle founded a leading newspaper and, after several years' service as a congressman, was elected senator in 1898 and president in 1903.

Armed with a strong personality, new ideas, and a genius for political organization, Batlle not only led a new administration but also launched a new era. He served twice as president, from 1903 to 1907 and from 1911 to 1915, and remained a dominant influence in Uruguayan politics long after his death in 1929. Batlle based his appeal to the electorate on moral force. He sought and won backing from

Courtesy of Organization of American States

José Batlle y Ordóñez—Uruguay's president from 1903 to 1907 and from 1911 to 1915—founded the liberal Colorado party newspaper *El Día* and instituted liberal democratic reforms.

Independent Picture Service

Named for the man who brought modern social legislation to the nation, Batlle Park in Montevideo is the home of this stadium, where full-capacity crowds throng the stands during soccer matches.

the nation's forgotten workers and a then-silent middle class—two groups not previously wooed by office seekers.

Under Batlle's leadership, armed politics gave way to electoral politics—though not without a fight. The fight was a Blanco rebellion, which lasted nearly a year, from its beginning on Christmas Day, 1903, to the rebel defeat on September 1, 1904. In putting down the insurrection, Batlle exercised firmness and persuasion. In the process, he gave Uruguayans a sense of purpose and a positive national morale. They began to believe that social progress and a better life for all could be achieved.

Batlle energetically promoted education, improved conditions among the nation's workers, and increased efficiency in public administration. During his years in office railways were built; ports were modernized; and waterworks, gas, electricity, and telephones were introduced. He emancipated his country from foreign exploitation and safeguarded free institutions.

By channeling the currents of change, Batlle was able to give reforms focus and sweeping force. At the same time, he held off radicals who wanted faster reform, Conservatives who wanted no reform at all, and dawdling politicians who were mainly interested in pocketing the rewards of office. As a result of his leadership, in the early 1900s Uruguay achieved social and economic goals that much of the world is still far from reaching today.

Under Batlle's influence a new constitution became effective in 1919. The constitution provided for a popularly elected president, a nine-member national council of administration, and a bicameral (two-house) congress. The congress also was equipped with a seven-member permanent commission that was empowered to act while congress was not in session. The Blancos did not oppose this new charter. It was hard for them to campaign against social security, workers' rights, and the breakdown of class divisions when the country was enjoying peace and prosperity.

Photo by Don Irish

Built in 1897, this Parisian-style building—with wrought-iron balconies and intricately colored vertical panels—adds subtle beauty to Eighteenth of July Avenue in Montevideo.

Photo by Don Irish

Prominently displayed on Uruguay's government buildings, the coat of arms dates from 1908. Framed by olive and laurel branches, the emblem displays scales, standing for justice; the fortress of Montevideo, standing for strength; the bull, representing abundance; and the horse, freedom.

The Mid-Twentieth Century

Following Batlle's principles, the government of Uruguay worked fairly smoothly until the Great Depression, which lasted from 1929 until the mid-1930s. During these years of extreme, worldwide economic decline, the normal procedure of government broke down. President Gabriel Terra quarreled with the National Council of Administration and was the object of impeachment proceedings by the congress. After using force to suppress his opposition, Terra dissolved both the council and the congress and for four years ruled as a dictator. In 1934 he persuaded the country to accept a new constitution, which provided for a representative and democratic form of government. The nation was headed by an elected president and assisted by a nine-member council of government—whose members were appointed by the president, not elected by the people.

This revised constitution worked well enough until the end of 1951, when the people voted to substitute for the president a nine-member executive body—the National Council of Government—under which the presidency rotated from one member to another, allowing the Colorado and Blanco parties to share power. Under this system, the Blancos won a national election in 1958 for the first time in 93 years.

Uruguay's economy began to decline during the 1950s. Inflation increased dramatically, and the country lost markets for its agricultural exports. At the same time, the cost of imports and of the nation's social programs increased. The National Council of Government proved unable to deal with these problems effectively.

Independent Picture Service

The presidential offices are housed in this impressive building on Montevideo's Plaza Independencia. The presidency of Uruguay has undergone a number of changes since the office was first established by the Constitution of 1830.

A huge celebration in 1930 commemorated the centennial of the construction of the capitol.

In 1960 Uruguayans marched in full-dress parade to welcome visiting U.S. president Dwight D. Eisenhower.

Tupamaro Terrorism

As Uruguay's economic problems increased in the 1950s and 1960s, a well-organized terrorist movement emerged. The Tupamaros—who took their name from Tupac Amarú, a rebellious Peruvian Indian of the late eighteenth century—presented a serious challenge to law and order. Many Uruguayans were surprised to see their country, known for its dedication to the peaceful resolution of differences, give birth to a secret, armed rebellion.

At the time there was general alienation and discontent among the nation's citizens. Although Uruguay had developed a notably advanced form of welfare state, money to support that system could no longer be counted on. Dissatisfaction and resentment had replaced popular expectations. In the midst of this negative climate, the Tupamaros at first achieved something of a Robin Hood reputation. They robbed banks and casinos and distributed some of their take to the poor. They also stole and exposed confidential records that revealed corruption in government and public administration. The sophistication of their operations, combined with skillful public relations, enabled the Tupamaros to recruit the sons and daughters of Uruguay's middle class.

Faced with the threat of the Tupamaros, Uruguayans in 1966 voted to replace the executive council—which had proved weak in countering the terrorist threat—with a presidential system. In that year the Colorados returned to power, placing in office General Oscar D. Gestido, a retired officer who had begun his military career at the age of 16. Although he died after just nine months in office, Gestido significantly increased the size and efficiency of Uruguay's police and armed forces, with substantial help from the United States.

Under the Colorado successors in office, all-out war against the Tupamaros developed. The Tupamaros changed their tactics and, to draw attention to their cause, turned to kidnapping and murder.

Success in suppressing the Tupamaros helped Uruguay's military to achieve popular acclaim and to emerge as the dominant force in the nation's government. In June 1973, still riding high in popular esteem, Uruguay's military leaders closed down the legislature and took control of the government—acting, as they announced at the time, to preserve the nation's newfound domestic tranquillity. For three years the military ruled through the device of a council of state dominated by the military. In 1977 the armed forces announced a timetable that called for the full restoration of democratic institutions by 1985, but they maintained tight control of the political process, and human rights abuses became a serious concern.

Finally, on March 1, 1985, Colorado party leader Julio Maria Sanguinetti took the oath of office for a five-year term along with the members of a new legislature. Both were elected by the Uruguayan people. Sanguinetti, a journalist by profession, knew that his ability to finish his elected term in office would depend on continued support from the nation's military leaders.

Uruguay's police and armed forces *(right and below)* were expanded and modernized during the 1960s to control the rise of terrorism by the Tupamaros.

Independent Picture Service

Presidents of the Western Hemisphere met at Uruguay's famous beach resort of Punta del Este in 1967.

Government

The modern structure of Uruguay's government dates from 1967, when a new constitution was adopted as a means of promoting the progress of a nation that had fallen into dire economic straits. The new constitution provided for a presidential system, with a president and vice president who are elected for five-year terms. In Uruguay the president serves as the supreme authority and acts with the advice of a 10-member council of ministers.

In order to provide a link between the president and the nation's legislature, ministers of the council may attend and speak at sessions of either house of the General Assembly—as the legislature is called—but they may not vote in proceedings there. Under the Uruguayan system, the president may not run for a second consecutive term.

The General Assembly, which makes the laws of Uruguay, consists of two houses: a senate and a chamber of deputies. The people elect the 30 members of the senate

at large—without regard to political districts—to five-year terms. The chamber of deputies has 99 members, who are elected to represent each of Uruguay's nine departments.

With legislative salaries generally low, members of both houses of the General Assembly often have another profession. As might be expected, there are frequent conflicts of interests when legislators who have private interests in various professions—such as banking or trade unions—attempt to represent these same groups on the floor of the assembly.

Uruguay's supreme court consists of a chief justice and four associate justices who all serve five-year terms and are appointed by the nation's General Assembly. Like the president and vice president, justices of the supreme court may not be immediately reappointed to another term of office—they must wait at least five years. Uruguay's top court decides on the constitutionality of all laws passed by the federal and local governments and appoints judges for all lower courts and all justices of the peace.

Each of Uruguay's departments has its own council with executive functions, as well as an assembly with legislative duties. All officers at the departmental and national levels are elected by the Uruguayan people. Everyone over 18 is eligible to vote. In recent years 80 to 90 percent of Uruguayan men and women have turned out to vote.

The department of Montevideo has a 65-member assembly and a 7-member council. The other departments have 31-member assemblies and 5-member councils. Towns within the departments are governed by a 5-member council that is appointed by the departmental council, with proportional representation from the nation's political parties.

Independent Picture Service

The Uruguayan government has attempted to provide the finest in medical care for the nation's citizens. One of the best-known medical facilities is the Hospital de Clinicas in Montevideo.

Independent Picture Service

Uruguayans who have taken an important part in affairs of the Western Hemisphere include José A. Mora, who served as secretary general of the Organization of American States from 1956 to 1968.

Independent Picture Service

Richly ornamented, the impressive entrance hall of Uruguay's capitol building contains murals that depict the country's history. Marble pillars support tall, graceful archways, giving the hall a light, airy feeling. Intricately patterned floors complete the decoration.

41

A vendor at a market in Montevideo sells a colorful variety of flowers.

Photo by Don Irish

3) The People

The absence of extremes of wealth or poverty in Uruguay gives the nation's 3.1 million people a basically middle-class outlook. Despite some economic hardships since the mid-twentieth century, most Uruguayans enjoy adequate food, housing, and medical care. The nation's cities have fewer slums than most Latin American countries, and only the poorest city dwellers lack electricity, running water, and sewers.

Emigration from Europe

That Uruguay should have a European flavor is not surprising, for 9 out of every 10 Uruguayans were either born in Europe or had parents or grandparents who were born there. Of these European descendants, almost 90 percent came from Spain or Italy, in about equal proportions. Italian immigrants—who, for the most part, came from major Italian cities—were easily assimilated into modern-day, middle-class Uruguay. This situation did not prevail with the Spanish newcomers, however, many of whom immigrated from impoverished rural areas of Spain. The nation's primary cultural traditions are Spanish, reflecting the heritage of the earliest immigrants. The universal language is Spanish—or, better said, the distinctively accented, Río-de-la-Plata variant of Spanish.

Many other European nationalities—including Portuguese, English, Irish, Welsh, French, German, Dutch, Greek, and Scandinavian—are represented in Uruguay's cosmopolitan population. Since the early nineteenth century, significant numbers of British have been settling in Uruguay, and this so-called Anglo-Uruguayan community exercises a strong influence in local affairs.

Blacks comprise less than 1 percent of Uruguay's population. They are about evenly divided between town and country. While there is no open discrimination against blacks, few are found in the upper ranks of government, business, or the professions.

The country's original inhabitants, the Charrúa Indians, have left behind only a legend of their existence—which included more than a century's resistance to Spanish and Portuguese colonizers. Today less than 10 percent of Uruguay's population can claim an Indian heritage, though Charrúa descendants are proud of their ancestry.

Photo by Don Irish

This statue, which graces a park in Montevideo, commemorates Uruguay's Indian heritage.

Spanish-style architecture is still common throughout much of Montevideo.

Photo by Don Irish

Religion

The majority of Uruguayans profess affiliation with the Roman Catholic Church, though they themselves are the first to say that they are casual about their religion. Protestantism, represented by many denominations and hundreds of congregations long present in Uruguay, has grown markedly in strength and influence in recent years.

Since the Constitution of 1919, church and state have been separated in Uruguay. The bond between the two was never very strong, however, except in early colonial times before the Jesuits were expelled. There is no patron saint, no national shrine of renown, nor any mass pilgrimage. Religious holidays have been renamed: Christmas is "Family Day" and Holy Week is "Tourism Week"—a holiday when virtually the entire population takes to the beaches, the hills, or the countryside, and public lodgings and campgrounds are filled

to capacity. Politically, the Roman Catholic Church makes use of the Christian Democratic party—a party that is relatively insignificant in Uruguay—as a vehicle for voicing its ideas and publicizing its objectives.

Communications

Uruguay is well served by the communications media. Nearly every Uruguayan listens to one of about 70 radio stations in the nation, 30 of them broadcasting from the capital city. Most of the population is reached by television stations that broadcast from the capital. Besides Uruguayan radio and television, the nation is served by stations transmitting from nearby metropolitan areas such as Buenos Aires in Argentina and Pôrto Alegre and São Paulo in Brazil.

Montevideo has several daily newspapers, with a combined circulation of approximately 400,000. The Blanco party's publication is *El País,* and the Colorado party publishes *El Día.* Other newspapers are generally, but not strongly, identified with political parties.

Education

Uruguayans are a well-educated people. As a nation, Uruguay shares with Argentina the highest level of educational attainment in South America. The two countries lead all South American countries in adult literacy and in the proportion of their children in school.

A Uruguayan tradition holds that a public education is the birthright of all children. The government operates free schools from kindergarten through college. This emphasis dates from the 1870s, when the remarkable educator José Pedro Varela inspired many young Uruguayans to become teachers. Varela infused the entire nation with enthusiasm to develop and improve the existing educational system. The Ministry of Culture, which has charge

Jackson Episcopal Church is one of numerous Protestant houses of worship in Montevideo.

An immigrant from Spain who has settled in Uruguay still proudly wears his Old World beret.

Neatly tilled plots surround the School of Agriculture at Sayago, a suburb of Montevideo.

These young boys and girls, seen at a party, live in a home for orphans. School is compulsory for all children between the ages of 5 and 14.

45

These Uruguayan children live in farm communities on the outskirts of Montevideo. Even in rural areas, school attendance is high.

of education, has long been accorded cabinet status.

There are two kinds of high schools in Uruguay. One leads to a diploma known as the *bachillerato,* approximately equivalent to the first two years of undergraduate school in the United States. The other offers vocational training in fields such as carpentry, electricity, radio repair, nursing, hospital administration, and automobile and heavy-machinery mechanics. In rural areas vocational schools teach animal husbandry, soil conservation, and dairy farming. Vocational training is administered as part of the Uruguayan Labor University, which operates about 74 different technical schools throughout the country. There are also special schools for the blind and the handicapped.

At the top of Uruguay's educational system is the University of the Republic, composed of several colleges—law and social sciences, medicine, engineering, architecture, chemistry and pharmacy, dentistry, economic sciences and administration,

veterinary medicine, and humanities and sciences. Most university studies take six years to complete and lead to a doctoral degree in a particular field.

The School of Engineering is housed in a modern building at the University of the Republic in Montevideo.

Like the cowboys of Uruguay's past, this farm worker enjoys chewing tobacco.

Rural Life

The people of the Uruguayan countryside tend to be hardworking, thrifty, and dedicated to traditional values. The nation's farms and ranches have historically provided the conservative Blanco party with its base of strength. In part, the conservatism of Uruguayan farmers and ranchers arises out of a familiar hostility between those living in the country and those residing in the city. Uruguayan farmers feel that they generate the major portion of the national income—which they believe is then spent wastefully by the soft, city-based bureaucrats.

This man owns a small farm near the community of San Bautista in the department of Canelones. Ninety percent of the farms in the departments surrounding Montevideo are family owned.

A mother and son who live in the country inspect their vegetable garden.

47

In Uruguay's mild climate, rural people often go barefoot and live in simple houses. They are much better off, however, than the impoverished farm laborers in many other Latin American countries, for they are literate and very well nourished.

In expressing beliefs of this nature, Uruguayan farmers are well spoken, generally well informed and forthright. In contrast to many of the campesinos (farm laborers) of other Latin American nations—who scratch out a poverty-level existence from worn-out, rocky soil—Uruguayan farmers till and ranch some of the most prosperous lands in South America. Well-fed and often well-educated, Uruguayan farmers and their families are productively self-employed.

The Gaucho

Uruguay's legendary gaucho—who is something like the stereotyped cowboy of North America's Wild West—is an idealized version of the real-life gaucho. Today's gauchos wear blue jeans, topcoats, and soft black hats with the brim upturned in the front. While horseback riding is still a popular sport in Uruguay, today's gauchos are more likely to drive a jeep or truck when working. Those who do ride horses probably mount a western-style saddle, rather than the sheepskin saddle of the rugged gaucho past. Many gauchos carry a transistor radio and a thermos of hot water for making maté (tea). They have also added vegetables to their once meat-heavy diet.

Although Uruguay's gaucho has clearly changed, the memory of the old-time gaucho—clad in a long woolen poncho, riding hard, and fighting with a facón (knife) at every opportunity—is still in the national consciousness. The traditional image of the South American gaucho was immortalized by José Hernández, an Argentine who over a century ago wrote the epic poem, *Martín Fierro*. Widely read in Uruguay as well as in Argentina, this epic has become a part of the national heritage. Parts of it have even been absorbed into the modern Spanish language, just as parts of Shakespeare's works and the King James version of the Bible have been assimilated into the English language.

This dairy farmer and his family are German-Swiss descendants who live near the city of Treinta y Tres.

Although few Uruguayan farm workers retain the traditional outfit, these gauchos still wear bombachas (baggy trousers), leather boots, and facons—short, daggerlike knives carried on the back of their belts.

Gauchos wearing traditional clothing "break" a horse for riding.

Literature

Although the earliest writers in Uruguay were shaped almost entirely by European styles, the late nineteenth century saw the development of a Uruguayan national style. One of the first contributors to this modern nationalist trend was José Alonso y Trelles, who wrote about gauchos and tried to reproduce their dialect.

The most important and influential Uruguayan writer is José Enrique Rodó, widely known and admired for his philosophical essay, *Ariel*. While the essay deals with the interaction between reason and spirit, it has been widely interpreted as symbolizing the conflict between a rich and materialistic United States and a poor but struggling and idealistic Latin America.

Outstanding among Uruguay's poets is Juan Zorrilla de San Martín. His epic poem *Tabaré,* published in 1888, depicts the victory of the human spirit—symbolized by the Spaniard—over the forces of nature—symbolized by the Charrúa. Among women poets who have achieved recognition are Juana de Ibarbourou and Delmira Augustini. Ibarbourou wrote of the parallel between the seasons of the year and the human seasons of youth, maturity, old age, and decay. Augustini has written of the joys of physical love.

Courtesy of Organization of American States

José Enrique Rodó, a Uruguayan man of letters, is best remembered for an essay entitled *Ariel,* which portrays the United States as a nation absorbed with materialism.

Independent Picture Service

At an open-air fiesta in rural Uruguay, gauchos and children gather around musicians.

Music and Art

Much Uruguayan folk music, which has been making a comeback in recent decades, centers around the familiar themes in gaucho legends. The country's earliest folk music arose from the lonely life of the gauchos, who improvised songs of love and adventure. Like Spanish folk songs, these songs followed the popular ballad form and were sung around the evening campfire to the accompaniment of guitars. The music gave rise to what has become Uruguay's national dance—the pericón. A round dance in triple time, the pericón is performed by couples and resembles the French minuet.

Uruguay's classical music from the nineteenth century is heavily influenced by opera from Italy—where most Uruguayan musicians are trained. The country's most famous composer, however, Eduardo Fabini, studied in Belgium. Often inspired by the serenity of the Uruguayan countryside, Fabini became known as a musical nationalist. Among the younger generation of composers and performers, Hector Tosar Errecart has been particularly successful. Tosar Errecart—a child prodigy who had composed several works by the age of 19—was recognized internationally in the 1950s for his neoclassical adaptation of gaucho folklore in *Danza Criolla*, or Creole dance. The government supports

50

In requesting a building permit for Casa Pueblo (People House), Uruguayan artist Carlos Páez Vilaró specified his desire to construct a "sculpture" big enough to live in. The unplanned construction of the handsome house was helped by curious visitors who donated doors, windows, and other building materials.

Courtesy of Eugenio Hintz

Photo by Museum of Modern Art of Latin America,
Organization of American States

Artist Carlos Páez Vilaró entitled this sculpture *Melchior,* after one of the three wise men present at the birth of Jesus. The structure is roughly three feet high.

both a national symphony orchestra and a ballet company.

Uruguay's first prominent painter was Juan Manuel Blanes, who gained fame for his paintings illustrating the nation's history. In the early twentieth century, José Cuneo was an outstanding impressionist painter, whose favorite subject was moonlit landscapes done in watercolors. Famous sculptors have included José Luis Zorrilla de San Martín—son of the poet Juan Zorrilla de San Martín—and José Belloni. Reflecting themes of Uruguay's gaucho past, Zorrilla de San Martín's *Monument to a Gaucho* and *The Last Charrúa* and Belloni's *Covered Wagon* grace Montevideo's parks.

One of Uruguay's best-known contemporary artists is Carlos Páez Vilaró, known in the United States for his 536-foot-long mural in the Pan American Union building in Washington, D.C. Páez is an artist of many talents—in addition to painting, he sculpts, writes poetry, and composes music. He has designed a fantastic structure near Punta del Este that is a sculpture, vacation house, and restaurant.

51

At a rodeo in Montevideo's El Prado Park, untamed horses challenge the skill and strength of Uruguay's gauchos.

Recreation

Montevideo offers year-round theater, opera, and ballet performances, as well as a great many sporting events. Horsemanship is a tradition in Uruguay, and horse racing and rodeos are very popular. Many Uruguayans participate in boating, swimming, and other water sports, as well as in tennis, golf, and basketball. By far the most popular sport in this sports-conscious country, however, is *futbol* (soccer). The two chief soccer clubs, the Peñarol and the Nacional, have fans as devoted as any in the world, and the Uruguayan teams have often won world championships.

All of Uruguay celebrates Carnival, the two-day festival before the beginning of Lent. During Carnival, parades with flowered floats and marchers in garishly colored masks and costumes fill the streets. Streamers and colored lights adorn the buildings. A *tablado*—a brilliantly decorated stage—is set up in each neighborhood, where painted musicians, clowns, dancers, and masked actors perform. At the end of Carnival, prizes are

Young people enjoy playing *futbol* (soccer), the nation's favorite sport, at a park in Montevideo.

awarded for the best tablado presentations.

Food

European influences are strong in the restaurants of Montevideo, many of which serve Italian and French cuisine. But typical Uruguayan dishes, like those of Argentina, reflect the country's gaucho past and meat-eating tastes. Especially popular is asado, barbecued beef or lamb rubbed with coarse salt and roasted on a spit over hot coals. A variation of this is asado con cuero, yearling beef roasted in its own hide.

Other meat dishes are *parrillada*—a mixture of grilled sausage, kidney, and liver—and *punchero,* meat boiled with chickpeas, bacon, and various vegetables. Popular snacks or appetizers are empanadas (little spiced meat pies). Coffee, tea, wine, and beer are consumed, but the national drink is maté—a tea brewed from a species of native holly. Farmers and ranchers customarily drink maté from a gourd, with a silver, strawlike tube called a bombilla.

Independent Picture Service

Tourists and upper-income residents dine and dance in Old World luxury and charm at Montevideo's Hotel Victoria Plaza. The restaurant offers a wide variety of meat, fish, vegetables, and fruit—all artfully prepared by skilled chefs.

This woman brews maté on the spot. At the base of her silver bombilla is an enlarged, perforated compartment in which she places the maté leaves. Hot water from a vacuum bottle is then poured into the gourd that holds the bombilla.

Independent Picture Service

Courtesy of Inter-American Development Bank

Workers at a meat-packing plant outside Montevideo prepare beef for local and foreign markets. The facilities of this plant have been modernized with the help of funds from the Inter-American Development Bank.

4) The Economy

Livestock raising and farming dominate the economic activities in Uruguay. Sales from meat, wool, and hides until recently accounted for about two-thirds of the nation's exports. Some 90 percent of the nation's total farming lands are devoted to raising animals, and the fortunes of the Uruguayan economy rise and fall with the fluctuations of world prices for meat and wool.

Uruguayans are personally involved in efforts to increase the nation's profits. When beef prices are high, or when the nation's treasury is depleted, Uruguayans are asked by their government to eat less beef, so that more of the nation's produc-

tion can be sold overseas. During these periods, called *vedas*—when it is also forbidden to sell beef in public places—Uruguayans must settle instead for substitutes such as lamb, liver, and sausage.

Most of the other items that figure importantly in Uruguay's export income —hides, maize (corn), wheat, citrus fruits, barley, rice, oats, sugar, tobacco, and linseed oil—are products of the land. The nation is making a firm effort to develop its manufacturing capacity, however, and now exports items such as textiles, cement, wines, and a growing line of processed foods. Uruguay's most important customers are the nations of the European

This new plant has enabled Uruguay to expand its production of cement. The complex—including its mill grinders and bank-financed silos—is located in Paysandú.

Milking is done by hand at the Benito Ramos dairy farm, where each worker milks 120 cows twice a day.

A Norwegian tanker unloads oil from Mexico through two large hoses. An underwater pipe transports the oil to a storage terminal on the mainland, a mile and a half away. It takes about 30 hours to unload an average-sized tanker, with divers periodically checking all underwater connections.

Economic Community—notably West Germany and Italy—as well as Argentina, Brazil, and the United States.

Declining Agricultural Earnings

Since the mid-1950s Uruguay has been troubled by economic stagnation. Agricultural markets for Uruguay's exports have steadily decreased because of global surpluses and extremely competitive tactics, such as cost controls. With dwindling investments in agriculture, Uruguay's farmers and ranchers have become less efficient producers.

A chain reaction adversely affecting Uruguayan farmers—which has also been experienced by farmers of industrialized nations—has set in. As farming revenue decreases, farmers are unable to pay their debts and the courts repossess what productive assets are left. Uruguayan farmers

Courtesy of Inter-American Development Bank

To promote the marketing of handicrafts and homemade products, Uruguay has established a nonprofit association of 18 cooperatives—like this one located in the town of Florida. One of the cooperative's members displays a vest that will be sold in Montevideo.

Courtesy of Inter-American Development Bank

Mario Gilberto Barrios Silva belongs to a milk-producers' cooperative near the city of Treinta y Tres, about 60 miles southwest of the Brazilian border and the same distance inland from the Atlantic coast. His four sons have joined him after helping with the afternoon milking. .

have been particularly hard hit by past sharp increases in the prices of petroleum and by the skyrocketing cost to maintain social programs that have been in place a long time.

From 1975 through 1986 Uruguay suffered a 40 percent decline in per capita income. With the stagnation of new investment in a country whose main attraction is land, Uruguay was suffering depression-era levels of unemployment by 1986. On top of this, the annual inflation rate in 1985 was over 65 percent. Uruguayans with university degrees were forced to sell handmade goods on the sidewalks of Montevideo to eke out a living.

Government—A Big Employer

In the past, Uruguayans looking for jobs turned to their government—a government that directly or indirectly employs about one-third of the nation's total work force. But recently, to satisfy its foreign creditors, Uruguay's government has been forced to trim the bloated rosters of ministries and regional services. Jobs in these nonessential areas had previously grown by leaps and bounds, giving rise to a popular Uruguayan refrain: "If it's not profitable, you can bet that the government is running it."

In Uruguay the theory seems to be that the government must provide a job for everyone, even when there is no job. Over

Courtesy of Inter-American Development Bank

A student at the Uruguayan Labor University learns how to operate a lathe while making a new shaft for a turbo lubrication pump. The pump will be used in a gas compressor at a petroleum refinery.

the years this philosophy has led to the government's acquisition of the railways and of industries such as electrical power, meat packing, petroleum, alcohol, and fishing. Most of these government-run businesses, however, are overstaffed and are forced to offer services or products at uneconomically low rates. In addition, numerous government-subsidized boards and commissions—many of them with overlapping authority and with legions of employees—were created to control rents

Courtesy of Inter-American Development Bank

In secondary cities like Treinta y Tres, milk is still delivered door-to-door by a horse-drawn cart. Here, Bolívar de los Santos pours milk he processed himself on a nearby dairy farm.

The Uruguayan government provides training in technical skills, such as the operation of machine tools.

tenure—they can be discharged only for the most severe neglect of duty, not for mere incompetence or inefficiency. The government's retirement system extends to an incredible number of Uruguayans. Nearly everyone can qualify for a pension, either in their own right or because a relative once worked for the government.

Uruguayans themselves are the first to criticize the shortcomings of their system. They put up with it because they are eager to make sure that a fair proportion of their friends and relatives are on the federal payroll. Because the government is such a big employer and because employees are often chosen for political reasons, Uruguayans are politically minded people.

Trade Unions

and prices, to oversee the nation's tourist business, and even to operate hotels and gambling casinos.

Furthermore, the benevolent Uruguayan government tightly protects its workers and their jobs. Uruguay has one of the most elaborate codes for civil service of any nation. Government employees enjoy

Uruguay's unions, which date from the 1890s, are strong and well organized, making their weight felt in the nation's political affairs. Recently, Uruguay's military-influenced government instituted a registration to bring the trade unions under democratic regulation. In so doing, the government hoped to curb chaotic conditions

In Minas employees and pensioners of a state-run union for electrical workers enjoy hotel and recreational facilities at a vacation-and-retirement park for union members.

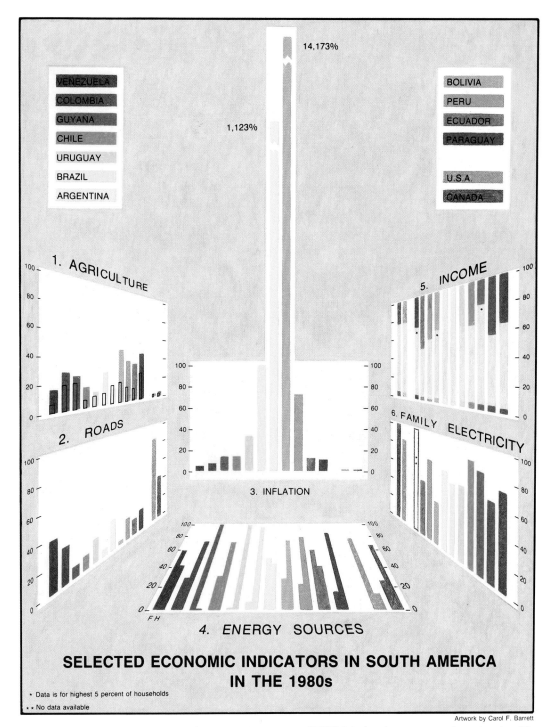

SELECTED ECONOMIC INDICATORS IN SOUTH AMERICA IN THE 1980s

* Data is for highest 5 percent of households

** No data available

Artwork by Carol F. Barrett

This multigraph depicts six important South American economic factors. The same factors for the United States and Canada are included for comparison. Data is from *1986 Britannica Book of the Year, Encyclopedia of the Third World, Europa Yearbook,* and *Countries of the World and their Leaders, 1987.*

In GRAPH 1—labeled Agriculture—the colored bars show the percentage of a country's total labor force that works in agriculture. The overlaid black boxes show the percentage of a country's gross domestic product that comes from agriculture. In most cases—except Argentina —the number of agricultural workers far exceeds the amount of income produced by the farming industry.

GRAPH 2 depicts the percentage of paved roads, while GRAPH 3 illustrates the inflation rate. The inflation figures for Colombia, Guyana, and Brazil are estimated. GRAPH 4 depicts two aspects of energy usage. The left half of a country's bar is the percentage of energy from fossil fuel (oil or coal); the right half shows the percentage of energy from hydropower. In GRAPH 5, which depicts distribution of wealth, each country's bar represents 100 percent of its total income. The top section is the portion of income received by the richest 10 percent of the population. The bottom section is the portion received by the poorest 20 percent. GRAPH 6 represents the percentage of homes that have electricity.

in Uruguay's economy, caused in part by some 700 union-called strikes per year since the 1960s.

In general, workers are not pressed to apply themselves diligently. Most government employees, for example, work only half a day. In the summer they work in the mornings, with the afternoons free for the beach. In the winter it is the other way around—they work in the afternoons in order to spend the chilly mornings by the fireside at home. Almost all workers—in offices as well as in factories, in private industry as well as in the government—have a long tea break in the afternoon.

Farm Workers

The work habits of Uruguay's government and union workers contrast greatly with those of the nation's farm workers. Industrious and intelligent, Uruguay's farm force compares well with that of any other nation of the Western Hemisphere.

Though much of Uruguay's farming is in the hands of a relatively small section of the landowning class, their workers are not subjected to the toil found among farm laborers elsewhere in Latin America. Producers of nutritious and highly valuable beef, Uruguay's farm workers take pride in their work. The nation's livestock are

Courtesy of Inter-American Development Bank

This farmer belongs to an agricultural cooperative near Arenales, about 130 miles northwest of Montevideo. He grows corn and sugar beets and raises a few cows.

extremely well cared for, as are the fields and pastures. A visit to a Uruguayan estancia (large farm) is a memorable experience —the work of the place is well organized, well supervised, and well carried out.

But if Uruguay is to overcome economic stagnation, it must invest heavily in new technologies to increase farm production

Independent Picture Service

Uruguay's cattle owners are often big businesspeople. Some of them, like this rancher, own large herds worth vast sums of money.

Some of Uruguay's vast wool production goes into making high-quality rugs. This woman is learning the trade at the Uruguayan Labor University.

and to upgrade the quality of its grasslands. Uruguay must also develop the industries necessary to process more of its meat and other foods if the nation is to profit from the conversion of these products into finished consumer goods.

Farm workers pour fertilizer into a hopper before spreading it over a field in which white clover has been planted. Fertilizer—essential in producing high-yielding crops—is an important part of Uruguay's farm-improvement plans. Recently the Uruguayan government has offered a variety of programs that encourage farmers to upgrade the quality of their grasslands.

Wool for foreign markets is carefully baled and loaded for shipment overseas. This cargo is headed for Boston, in the United States.

Transportation

Uruguay has a well-developed system of highways. The most important highway leads west out of Montevideo to Colonia, on the Río de la Plata, before swinging west and north to pass Mercedes, a major market city, and Fray Bentos, hub of the meat-packing industry. The road then goes on to Paysandú (a port on the Uruguay River for oceangoing ships), Salto (a port for coastal shipping), and eventually Artigas on the Brazilian border.

East from Montevideo, another major highway leads to Chuy, a small town on the Brazilian border. This highway—along with the section of highway out of Montevideo that links the nation with Buenos Aires—is fast becoming a major commercial artery within Uruguay. It is also part of the most heavily traveled land route on the east coast of South America. The highway connects six major cities—Rio de Janeiro, São Paulo, Curitiba, Pôrto Alegre,

Courtesy of Inter-American Development Bank

Courtesy of Inter-American Development Bank

A new international bridge *(top left)* **spans the Uruguay River, linking Argentina and Uruguay. Nearby, the Salto Grande hydroelectric power plant** *(above)* **was built jointly by the two countries.**

Montevideo, and Buenos Aires. First-class buses keep to split-second schedules along this 1,000-mile-long run from Rio de Janeiro to Buenos Aires, as do big semi-trailers carrying products to and from the major urban markets. Providing Uruguay with a major opening for trade and commerce with the adjoining South American countries, this east-coast corridor is highly valued.

From Montevideo, other good roads lead into the interior of the country, enabling the transport of farm produce and livestock back to the capital. One of these roads runs due north from the capital, passing through the sizable towns of Florida, Durazno, Paso de los Toros, and Tacuarembó, before reaching the Brazilian frontier at Rivera. Another swings northwest from the capital, linking several agricultural towns before running north near the Argentine border through Paysandú, Salto, and Bella Unión.

Courtesy of David Mangurian

These extension agents encourage Uruguay's numerous family farmers to diversify their production. The government provides credits for those willing to establish vineyards or to grow soybeans and other crops for which world demand is high.

The Future

Many young Uruguayans have taken advantage of the highways to seek employment elsewhere, across the borders in the bustling cities of Brazil and Argentina, where the employment opportunities for well-educated Uruguayans are plentiful. By 1986, amid continuing economic stagnation at home, from 300,000 to 500,000 Uruguayans—nearly one-sixth of the total population—were living abroad.

Since the restoration of democracy on March 1, 1985, some of these young Uruguayans have returned home to participate in the reenergizing of their once-prosperous nation. With substantial assistance from abroad, Uruguayan leaders today are promoting long-range programs to reactivate Uruguay's economy. There is a new realism in the land as Uruguayans discover that solutions to their problems will not be achieved quickly or without pain. But there is optimism, too, that Uruguay—a

Courtesy of Inter-American Development Bank

An official of the Inter-American Development Bank (left) meets with a Uruguayan supervisor to discuss the flow of traffic between Montevideo and the cities and towns in the interior of Uruguay. The improvement project includes building 12 bridges and viaducts and 2 interchanges.

nation blessed with a homogeneous population and bountiful land resources—will again find a way to achieve self-fulfillment for its people.

Index

17397